T0113683

The

Naked Truth

Paulette Lewis-Brown

authorHOUSE®

AuthorHouse™
1663 Liberty Drive
Bloomington, IN 47403
www.authorhouse.com
Phone: 833-262-8899

Published by AuthorHouse 07/25/2022

ISBN: 978-1-6655-6571-4 (sc)
ISBN: 978-1-6655-6570-7 (e)

Print information available on the last page.

This book is printed on acid-free paper.

Chapter 1

WHAT IF JESUS SAYS THAT THE UNIVERSAL PUZZLE IS NOT COMPLETE WITHOUT PAULETTE. WOULD YOU LISTEN TO THIS NOTION OR WOULD YOU MAKE IT A COMMOTION.

SOMETIMES WE ASKED OURSELVES, WHERE'S LIFE TAKING US. DO WE ALWAYS NEED A DR TO EVALUATE OUR BRAIN, OR DO WE NEED A SCIENTIST TO PUT A MICROSCOPE INTO ACTION FOR A LOOK IN THE FUTURE. WHILE THERE'S NO GUESSING FACTOR IN EVERY DNA, LABORATORIES ARE JUST A SCOPE. AND A RAY OF SUNSHINE.

VITAMIN-D IS SUCH A BLESSINGS, NO WONDER EVERYONE WAS BORN NAKED. CHILDREN ARE A GIFT ON EARTH. EVERY CHILD IS IMPORTANT, NO ONE SHOULD BE LEFT BEHIND, REGARDLESS OF THEIR CULTURE. STAYING STRONG IS STRONG, BUT MAYBE NOT STRONG ENOUGH. THE WORLD NEEDSA SHOULDER TO LEAN ON, HIS NAME IS JESUS. HE'S THE ONLY PERFECT ONE.

PAULETTE IS A SERVANT, WHO WOULD NEVER GIVE UP HOPE. HER FAITH IS A VESSEL FILLED WITH PURE RUNNING WATER. RAIN IS A BLESSINGS REGARDLESS OF THE STORMS, HURRICANE, TORNADOES WE FACES.
NATURE IS A TREE, THAT GROWS FROM WITHIN.

NURTURE EVERY GIFTED SPIRIT, THEN WATCH IT GROW.
LIFE IS A TRUE DREAM.

IT'S NO SECRET THAT WE WERE ALL BORN NAKED. EXPLORE
LIFE JOURNEY WITH A SMILE.
BLESS EACH OTHER ALONG LIFE'S JOURNEY.
IT'S OKAY AND SAFE TO PRAY 🏰 DAILY.
JESUS BREAD WILL ACCOMMODATE ALL.
FEAR NOT OF THE UNKNOWN. COVID-19 IS
WATCHING YOU WATCHING ME. KEEP THE ENVIRONMENT
STREAKY CLEAN. MONITOR EVERY HEARTBEAT, THE PUMP
NEEDED IS LOVE.
STRATEGICALLY WATCH THE AORTA RELAX IN PEACE, WITH
A MIND OVER MATTER REGIME.

Chapter 2

FINDING BALANCE, WILL NOT BE EASY
EVERY HOUSEHOLD NEEDS A GUIDE.
LEAD WITH FAITH, BUT STILL ASK JESUS
FOR AN OPEN MINDED KEY 🔑.
WELCOME STRANGERS WITH OPEN ARMS
JESUS MAKES NO MISTAKES. LOVE IS CONTAGIOUS AND
FREE. EXPLORE ALL AVENUES AS LONG AS YOU BELIEVE.
TRUST YOUR GUT FEELINGS. IT'S ALWAYS SAFETY FIRST.

THE NAKED TRUTH IS LINED UNDERNEATH THE SKIN,
RAINBOW PROMISES WILL RUN WILED, BUT CAN ONLY BE
FULFILLED BY ONE.
THERE WILL BE NO MORE FLOOD, SAYS FATHER GOD SON.
THE BIBLE DOESN'T LIE. IT WILL BE THE NUMBER ONE
BOOK UNTIL ETERNITY.
SO I AM GRATEFUL THAT JESUS SPIRIT LIVES IN ME.

SOUND THE FREEDOM BELL, START THE ROLL CALL, SEND
OFF THE ALARM.
EVERY FAMILY IS BLESSED WITH A GIFTED CHILD. IDENTIFY
THAT SOUL AND PROTECT HIM OR HER, FROM THIS
WICKED WORLD. AMERICA SAFETY NET IS LIKE A FAILED
DISASTER PLAN.

EVERYONE LOOKING IN THE MIRROR. YET THE BLAME
COULD BE CAST DOWN ON A INNOCENT GIFTED CHILD.
THIS'S WHEN FAITH KICKS IN WITH THE MOST POWERFUL
ANGELS TO PROTECT AND SERVE.

JAMAICA IS KNOWN FOR THEIR CRAZY ONE LOVE, NO
PROBLEM CHILDHOOD DREAMS
THEIR ABILITY TO GIVE UP, IS NEVER AN OPTION. FAITH IS
WHAT MOST CARIBBEAN RUNS ON. THEY CAN NEVER RAN
OUT OF O2.
JESUS SUPPLY ALL NEEDS.
NOW THIS'S THE NAKED TRUTH. FEEL FREE TO STUDY THE
JAMAICAN CULTURE. PAULETTE IS CHOSEN FTOM THE
BOTTOM OF THE BARREL.
SMILE AND ENJOY THIS NEW ERA. IT'S CALLED FREEDOM.
NOW JESUS SEND DOWN THE RAIN.
THE RAIN IS THE MOST POWERFUL BLESSINGS YET. EVERY
RAIN DROPS SYMBOLS A LIFETIME
OF WHAT IS YET TO COME. FAITH, FAMILY AND A FEW
FRIENDS TO CELEBRATE LIFES JOURNEY.
ENDURE THE PAIN AND SUFFERING FROM THE HANDS
OF DOUBTERS, TODAY YOU'RE STRONGER THAN BEFORE.
EMBRACE THE INVISIBLE ☺ WELCOME EVERY HEART WITH
OPEN ARMS. EVERYONE NEEDS LOVE FROM AN ANGEL. I AM
NO MOTHER THERESA, BUT SISTER PAULETTE FROM WAY
YONDER.

Chapter 3

IF WE FOCUS ONLY ON THE MOON, WE WILL
FALL AMONGST THE STARS. LEAVING A VAST RAY
OF SUNSHINE WIDE OPEN WITH LOTS OF IDEAS
BOUNCING OFF BLUE MOUNTAIN PEAK.
THE NAKED TRUTH IS AN OPEN BOOK, YOU'RE
APPRECIATED BY THE POWERFUL MAN
UPSTAIRS. JESUS WORKS FROM WITHIN, HE
WANTS EVERYONE TO FIND HAPPINESS.

HAPPINESS IS NOT ALWAYS VISIBLE, SOMETIMES
WE NEED A MICROSCOPE 🔬 TO VIEW THIS
SPECTACULAR MOMENT. EVERYONE
NEEDS ARE DIFFERENT, DNA PLAYS A VITAL
PART, IN FINDING HAPPINESS, SCOPE THE VINE
OF THE FAMILY TREE. PRAYER IS STILL THE
NUMBER ONE 💊 MEDICINE FOR HEALING.
WHEN I CLOSE MY EYES, I MEDITATE AND
ZOOM INTO THE NAKED TRUTH.

BE CURIOUS, BE WISE, BE YOUR FULL
POTENTIAL, EXPAND YOUR HORIZONS
BE DRIVEN BY THE WARMTH OF SUCCESS
STEERING YOU IN THE FACE. KEEP IN MIND
A MOTTO SO STRONG AND CLEAR. NO ONE

IS AN ISLAND AND NO MAN STANDS ALONE.
JESUS WILL GUIDE THE RIGHT PEOPLE TO YOU.
KEEP IT REAL THAT NATURE VALLEY COULD NEVER
BE REPLACED, ONE CLUE. OUR LOYAL FURRY FRIENDS
ARE A TRUE BASE. EVERY HOUSEHOLD NEEDS A FOUR
LEGGED FAMILY. SMILE! LIFE IS A LONG JOURNEY
WITHOUT DOGGY MOLLY. RIP MY DEAREST ANGEL.

TRUE LOVE NEVER REALLY DIES, MEMORIES LIVES
ON. THE WORLD FACES SO MANY CRISES.
FAMILIES ARE EXHAUSTED WITH STRESS BEYOND
EVERY SCOPE OF PRACTICE. DOCTORS ARE BAFFLED
BY MIRACLES AND NEW BEGINNINGS, SCIENTISTS
ARE GOING BACK TO THE MICROSCOPIC MENTALITY
WITH ROOM TO LOOK BEYOND SCIENCE. AGAIN THIS'S
THE NAKED TRUTH, IT'S ALSO AN OPEN BOOK.
INTROVERTS AND EXTROVERTS ARE LEARNING
FROM EACH OTHER. LIFE IS BEYOND A DREAM.
ALWAYS BELIEVE IN YOUR INNER SELF.

Chapter 4

JESUS LOOKS OUT FOR THE WORLD,
BUT HE PAYS SPECIAL ATTENTION TO THOSE
WHO NEEDS HIM THE MOST. THE GIFTED ONES
WHO IN MOST CONVERSATIONS WERE NEVER GIVEN A
CHANCE TO BE HEARD. JESUS SPEAKS FOR THE NEGLECTED
ONES. HE'S BEHIND EVERY SCENE STRATEGICALLY
TAKING NOTES OF INJUSTICE. THE NAKED TRUTH
IS RELATED TO DREAMS FROM BEYOND THE SKIES,
YES ITS AN OPEN BOOK WRITTEN BY AN ANGEL.

GENIUS INVISIBLE WALL, AN OVER ACHIEVER STILL
INVISIBLE IN AMERICA. SO JESUS SPIN THE HOOK AND OPEN
A GENIUS INVISIBLE WALL SHOW, OPERATING FROM A BOOK.
GIVING THE SPACE TO BE AN ANCHOR FOR EVERY
BROKEN HEARTS WHO ENJOY NATURE.
JAMAICA WILL TAKE CREDIT FOR THIS ROOT.
IT WILL ALSO BE A SCOPE IN THIS IDEA.
WHY DID JESUS TRUST A BORN JAMAICAN TO BE THE
RECIPIENT OF SUCH POWERFUL DREAMS. GOOGLE THE
CHURCH WITH THE DREAM CENTER, WHY DID JESUS
OPEN THIS DOOR, THEN CLOSE IT WITH HIS IDEA.

THE FUTURE WILL BE AN OPEN BOOK.
CHURCHES WILL FACE TRIALS AND TRIBULATIONS,
LETS CALL IT CRISIS WITHIN
CRISIS ON TOP OF CRISIS. POLICIES AND
PROTOCOLS ARE TAMPERED WITH. FIELDERS
ARE EXHAUSTED AND HEAVY HEARTED.
MONEY IS ON THE TABLE, BUT NO ONE
WANTS TO TOUCH IT. JESUS AMAZING GRACE
SPREAD THE NATION. HAVE MERCY ON EVERY
SOUL, INCLUDED IN AN ANGEL PRAYER. SEND THE
HURRICANE AND TORNADO TO WASH AWAY ALL
SINS. SPRING TRUE LOVE FROM WITHIN. SEND US
PEACE TO WIPE AWAY OUR TEARS. SHALOM.

WHILE OUR FAITH IS HOLDING ON TO THE STRONGEST
ANCHOR, OUR HOPE SOMETIMES STRUGGLES TO STAY
ON PAR, FAMILIES ARE MISSING IN ACTION, FRIENDS
ARE HIDING UNDER FRICTIONS, ONLY THE WISE WILL
MONITOR THEIR PULSE AND BLOOD PRESSURE IN
THE MIDDLE OF NOWHERE. LIFE IS A POWERHOUSE
FILLED WITH LIGHTS. FOLLOW AND FREE YOUR MIND.
FREEDOM IS TRULY FREEDOM. ASK THE MAN UPSTAIRS
TO GUIDE YOUR FOOTSTEPS. HE'S NOT INVISIBLE,
TALK TO HIM. HIS NAME IS JESUS. HE KNOWS MY
NAME. EVERYONE IN THE WORLD IS BLESSED.
THIS'S NO TEST, IF YOU ONLY BELIEVE IN FAITH.

Chapter 5

EVERYONE JOURNEY IS DIFFERENT
SOME PEOPLE WILL BRAND IN ON A GURNEY
JESUS RELEASE THE SAFETY BELT, TO YOU IT
MIGHT BE INVISIBLE ☺. WHO GOD BLESS NO
ONE CAN CURSE. LOOK AROUND, FIRE, THEN
THE STORMS OF LIFE, PUT OUT THE BLAZE.
EXTRAORDINARY CIRCUMSTANCES STILL FILL THE AIR, ARE
WE ASLEEP OR IS COVID-19 STILL HERE UNDER THE SHEETS,
IS UNIVERSAL PRECAUTION STILL A PRACTICE OR A BREACH.
COULD WE SEE WEARING MASK A FOREVER TASK. ONLY
JESUS HAS THE ANSWER, AGAIN FREEDOM IS THE GLITCH
THAT CAN OPEN EVERY OPEN MIND IN THE FUTURE.
WAKE UP AND SEE CHANGE. WE'RE NOT BLIND.

STOP MY POEMS ARE TALKING ANOTHER POWERFUL
BOOK, WRITTEN BY AN INVISIBLE ANGEL, SO IS WALKING
POETS TREE, DON'T SOUND THE ALARM, DOCTORS WILL
LEARN FROM POETRY PACEMAKER, SEARCHING FOR THE
BUTTERFLY TECHNIQUE, TAKE A MOMENT TO BREATHE,
JESUS IS THE NUMBER ONE GURU IN MARKETING, WHY
WOULDN'T YOU TRUST HIM TO MONITOR AND CONTROL
YOUR MONEY. HE'S THE ONLY ONE WITH YOUR BEST
INTEREST AT HEART. MOST PEOPLE ARE STARS, WHO

FOCUS ON THE LIME LIGHT, BUT THERE ARE ALSO GENIUS
INVISIBLE WALLS WHO HIDES BEHIND THEIR IDEAS.
JESUS KNOWS THEM BY NAME. AMERICA TENDS TO HIDE
THOSE PEOPLE FOR THEIR SPECIAL NEEDS PROJECT.
WHY AMERICANS LIE AND THINK THEY CAN
GET AWAY WITH IT? YES THIS'S ALSO ANOTHER
BOOK THAT'S ON JESUS MARKETING LIST.

POEMS WILL BE SOLD IN LOTS,
STOCKS, BONDS AND SHARES WILL KNOW MY NAME.
COINS SALE WILL HIT THE ROOF. THERES ALREADY A
WRITTEN POEM STANDING IN PLAIN SIGHT. THE WORLD
WILL FACE A SHOCK WAVE, LOOK TO THE STRONG
TO SURVIVE. FAITH IS EVERYTHING, SO IS POETRY.
LOOK, LISTEN AND FEEL, SURVIVE ON YOUR OWN WILL.
THE WORLD BELONGS TO EVERY FAMILY, DON'T FIGHT
OVER JESUS MONEY, TRUE SONG WRITTEN BY AN ANGEL.

WHY IS SUSPENSE LINGERING IN MIDAIR.
JESUSISMYPWOWPWOW WAS CREATED FOR THE GIFTED1.
ITS A TRUE BOOK, SO DON'T PLAY ONE AGAINST THE OTHER
FOR A FOOL, OOPS THAT WORD ESCAPES THROUGH THE
CRACKS OF THE IMPERFECT WORLD. JUST BE COOL.
ENJOY THE SUN AND ITS RAYS, THE NAKED TRUTH IS ALL
OVER THE PLACE, SURVIVE ON A GIFTED SLATE. LOVE
UNTIL THERE'S MORE THAN ENOUGH LOVE LEFT TO GIVE.

MARRIAGE IS STILL A BOND, NO ONE SHOULD
TRY TO BREAK. TRUST THE ONE WHO JESUS
TRUSTED WITH YOUR HEART. PRAYER FOR THE
GAYS, JESUS LOVES EVERYONE IN THE WORLD.

WHO AM I TO JUDGE. I HAVE NO DEGREE IN
THE JUDGEMENT ZONE. SO I LOOK AT JESUS
LOOKING AT ME. THEN WE SMILE AND SAY.
FREEDOM IS A LEMON TREE. SIP WITH WATER
TO BE AN OVERCOMER. WELCOME THE
NEW YOU. MEDITATION IS A CLUE.

Chapter 6

THESE ARE FACTS, PRAYER IS THE NUMBER ONE MEDICINE.
JESUS IS MY MARKETING DIRECTOR, HE CONTROLS
ALL SALES ON THE ABUNDANCE OF BOOKS WRITTEN
HIS GIFTED ANGEL. JESUS IS MY POWER OF ATTORNEY,
YES HE'S MY DOCTOR MY LAWYER IN AMERICA.
WHEN PEOPLE FAILED ME, JESUS LIFT ME
UP OUT OF THE GUTTER THAT PEOPLE LIES
TRIES SO HARD TO KEEP ME THERE.
GRATITUDE IS MY DAILY BREAD, CHURCH IS
NOW IN MY HEART. DON'T ASK ME TO TRUST
A PASTOR, JESUS IS ALSO MY COUNSELOR, HE
LISTENS TO ME, AND LOOK ME IN THE EYES.

JESUS IS MY INVESTIGATOR, EVEN THOUGH
HE ALREADY KNOWS EVERYTHING THING. HE
ALERTS ME AND COME THROUGH MY CHANNEL
PAULETTE THERE'S ONLY ONE 🎵 OF YOU LEFT.
SO SAFETY FIRST IS ALWAYS A FIRST COMMANDMENT
BEST. WHEN AMERICA FAILED TO PROTECT YOU, LOOK
FOR ME, I WILL BE RIGHT BY YOUR SIDE. STANDING
FIRM, WITH A MICROSCOPIC LENSES BRIGHTER THAN
THEIR LIES. HUMBLE YOURSELF, LET ME LEAD.

THE NAKED TRUTH IS HEALING, IT'S BOOK #15
YET AMERICANS ARE STILL WONDERING WHO YOU ARE.
TWO TARGET SPEEDING TICKETS WAS GENERATED BY
POLICE IN 2021. YOU WERE STRATEGICALLY TARGETED
ON THE NIGHT SHIFT, YET THIS UNCOVERED
TRUTH IS STILL HIDING AND WATCHING YOU FROM
A FAR. JESUS IS COVERING HIS MOST POWERFUL
ANGEL, WITH WRITING ✍ TO PROTECT HER WELL-
BEING, AND HEALING EVERY SCAR FROM
WITHIN.
WHY AMERICANS BLAMES THE WORLD FOR BEING
PARANOID, WHEN THEY ARE THE ONLY COUNTRY WHO
WASTE JESUS MONEY IN THIS AREA. WHERE ARE ROOTS
AND CULTURE, WHERE ARE DIFFERENT UPBRINGING
AND SENSE OF HUMOR STANDS IN THE FUTURE.
WHO'S BLAMING WHO, WHEN SOMETHING
IS FABRICATED AND MADDISON IS NOT JUST A
JOKE, BUT REAL LAUGHTER. LET'S ENJOY JESUS
FREE PIZZA. LET'S EXPAND TOGETHER.
LETS CELEBRATE THE TWO IN ONE MASK AS A
DAILY TASK. EVERYONE IS A WINNER, BUT THERE'S
ONLY ONE 🔑 GENIUS INVISIBLE WALL.
LET'S TAKE A BREAK, THEN GEAR UP FOR THE 7th AND
LAST CHAPTER. SHINE THE LIGHT ON THE 15 BOOKS
THAT JESUS WILL BE MARKETING. FEEL FREE TO
WELCOME ME AND MY SPECIAL PAULETTE CHAIR 🪑.

Chapter 7

WHEN JESUS TOOK ON THIS TASK TO BE MY MARKETING
DIRECTOR, HE KNOWS THAT IT WOULD BE A PIECE OF
CHEESE CAKE. SO I ATE THAT THOUGHT WITH A SMILE.
HOW IS IT HUMANLY POSSIBLE THAT I WAS SO BRAVE TO
TAKE THIS INVISIBLE ROUTE. PATIENCE IS A VIRTUE, PLAYS
OVER AND OVER AGAIN IN MY HEAD. THEN I VISION JESUS
SOUNDING THE TRUMPET, TO EVERYONE IN THE WORLD.
THE KING IS COMING, PUT ON YOUR SCARLET ROBE.
JESUS ROYALTY LINES EVERY DNA, BE HAPPY IN YOUR
OWN SKIN, COMPLIMENT YOURSELF. PAULETTE IS NOT
LAST IN THE SUCCESS LINE, BECAUSE JESUS JUST TURN
THE LINE AROUND. BELIEVE IN YOURSELF FIRST.
LOOK TOWARDS THE FUTURE.
FATHER GOD HAS GIVEN HIS SON JESUS TO
GUIDE OUR SENSIBILITY, BE OPEN MINDED.
THE WORLD IS LIKE AN ELASTIC BAND
WE CAN STRETCH IT IN ANY DIRECTION,
AND THAT'S THE NAKED TRUTH.

THESE FIFTEEN BOOKS ROOTS ARE FROM JAMAICA,
AMERICA ACCOMMODATE JESUS ANGEL, BUT THEY
NEVER REALLY WELCOME HER WITH OPEN ARMS.
THERE'S ALWAYS DOUBT FLOATING AROUND IN

MID-AIR WITH NO STRINGS ATTACH. SO FAITH TOOK
OVER AND CONTROL THE BORDER AND WALLS.
NOW TODAY THESE BOOKS ARE READY LIKE
FREDDIE. SMILE IN THE UNIVERSAL MIRROR O.
LOOK AHEAD, ONLY THE PAST IS IN THE REAR VIEW
MIRROR. ORDER THESE BOOKS IN ABUNDANCE, EVERY
COUNTRY NEEDS TO REPENT AND SOLELY TRUST JESUS.
FIND THESE BOOKS WHEN LIFE KNOCKS YOU
DOWN, JUMP UP, TAKE A DEEP BREATH THEN START
LIFE OVER AGAIN. AMERICA ARE YOU READY?.
STANDING OVATION FOR THESE FIFTEEN BOOKS.

1- STOP MY POEMS ARE TALKING
2- WALKING POET'S TREE
3- JAMAICAN POETRY
4- POETRY PACEMAKER
5- GOLDEN PALM TREE
6-GENIUS INVISIBLE WALL
7- DREAMS FROM BEYOND THE SKIES
8- PLANT THIS DIAMOND
9- HOSPICE FOR OUR FURRY FRIENDS
10-WHY AMERICANS LIE AND THINK THEY
CAN GET AWAY WITH IT.
11-JESUSISMYPWOWPWOW
12 - JESUS ROYALTY
13- JESUS INVISIBLE ART
14- FAITH ON THE BULLY.
15- THE NAKED TRUTH.

MARKETING IS DEMONSTRATING THAT JESUS
HAVE THE ENTIRE WORLD IN HIS HANDS. ONLY
TIME WILL TELL THE MOMENT IN TIME.
START YOUR V8 ENGINE, THE ECONOMY WILL
RISE, FROM AN ANGLE NO ONE SAW COMING.

LETS JUST CALL THIS METHOD SEVEN LINER
POETRY BOOSTER. LIFE IS AN OPEN BOOK 📖.
YOUR CHAPTER IS ALREADY WRITTEN.
NOW ITS YOUR TIME TO WELCOME THE ONE YOU MAKE
INVISIBLE ALL THESE YEARS. CHEERS!. ALL CHURCHES
WILL OPEN A DREAM CENTER, INVITE PAULETTE CHAIR,
IT'S OKAY TO TAKE THIS NOTE TO THE ALTAR.
SHARE THE BREAD AND HONEY 🍯 AND PLEASE
STOP FIGHTING OVER JESUS MONEY. THERE'S
ENOUGH FOR EVERY FAMILY TREE.
SHARE THE WEALTH AND REMOVE ALL CRISES.
LOVE FROM WITHIN, JESUS IS THE GENIUS IN
MARKETING, SHARE WITH THE WORLD PERSEVERANCE,
VICTORY IN JESUS, AND LORD HAVE MERCY ON
THE WORLD. HEAL AND PROTECT US. SHALOM.

LIFE IS A TREE
FEED IT FROM THE ROOT UP
FREEDOM IS FREE, SO WATERING
THIS TREE IS EVERYONE'S DUTY
BREATHE IN AND FIND YOURSELF.
EVERYONE WAS BORN NAKED FOR
A REASON. EXHALE AND BE HAPPY.
ENJOY ALL FOUR SEASONS. LET GO
AND EXPRESS YOURSELF, TRUE NATURE
LIVES ON FOREVER. Dearest Moss.

JESUS IS THE ONLY OXYGEN WE NEED
USED HIM WISELY, HE'S LISTENING.
POLLUTION IN THE AIR, CRISIS IN HIGH
GEAR. HAVE NO FEAR, FATHER GOD IS
HERE. HEALING IS ON THE FRONT BURNER
INVITE HOPE AND GRACE TO COME OVER.
FAITH WILL PROVIDE THE SHELTER.
PRAYER IS SERVING FOR DINNER. SMILE
AND BREATHE EASY. LIFE IS SCOPE OF PRACTICE,
PRACTICE, PRACTICE, PRACTICE.
GRATITUDE TO EVERYONE WHO GRADE THIS O2.

Write Me a Poem Jesus
One to Sustain my Dignity.
Write Me a Poem Jesus
One to Relief my Pain.
Heal from within my
Broken Spirit. Use the
Left over Tissue to Patch
Up my Heart.
Write me a Poem Jesus.
This's A New Beginning
Give the World a new Start.
America & Jamaica
Together as one Unit.
Shalom.

THIS BRAIN HAS BEEN THROUGH
THE VALLEY OF THE SHADOW OF
DEATH, IT WAS BEATEN DOWN BY
PEOPLE LIES. THIS BRAIN CANNOT
SEE COLOR, BORDERS OR WALLS.
THIS BRAIN WAS STRATEGICALLY
PLACE IN YOUR PATH, JESUS IS
THE ONLY FORCE BEHIND THIS BRAIN.
HE STEPPED IN SO THIS BRAIN WOULD
NEVER WALK ALONE. AMERICA THIS BRAIN
IS NOW AN AMERICAN EAGLE, NURTURE THIS
BRAIN, LIKE IT WAS YOUR OWN. START FROM
GROUND ZERO, REBUILD AN AMERICAN EAGLE
WITH AN HUMMINGBIRD BELLY. SMILE! THIS
BRAIN WILL BRING OUT THE HERO IN YOU.
ACCOMMODATE AND WELCOME THIS BRAIN.
THIS BRAIN IS ALIVE, NOW THE WORLD CAN
READ THE NAKED TRUTH. A SLATE
FROM THIS BRAIN. SHALOM.

NOTHING IS SET IN STONE
EVERYTHING IS SUBJECT
TO CHANGE.
LIVE LIFE AND ENJOY
EVERY MOMENT.

THIS WORLD IS IN CRISIS
BUT THIS SHOULD NOT
BE THE SAME FOR YOU.
KNOW YOUR WORTH AND
TAKE A STEP FORWARD.
JESUS IS IN FRONT OF YOU.
NOTE FROM AN ANGEL.

JESUS INVISIBLE ART
IS NOW AN AMERICAN
EAGLE, LEAVING THE
HUMMINGBIRD BEHIND
WAS'NT EASY. JESUS
DNA  STILL BUILD AND
WORKS FROM WITHIN.
EVERY SOUL NEEDS
HEALING. EVERY HEART 🖤
NEEDS PEELING. 🔒
MOMENT OF SILENCE
WITH THE ONE WHO
SURVIVE EVERY ORDEAL.
YET STILL PROUD TO
BE AN AMERICAN,
CELEBRATING TRUE FREEDOM 🎹

AN ASCP PHLEBOTOMIST PRAYER
JESUS HELP ME TO FOLLOW
POLICIES AND PROTOCOLS DAILY.
APPLIED SAFETY NET WHENEVER
POSSIBLE. BE MY MENTOR, AND
BRING ME CLOSER TO MY CONSCIENCE
DAILY. EXCELLENCE IS THY NAME.
BLESS MY TECHNIQUE FROM THE GROUND
UP ⬆ AMEN 🏛 📢 PLB

MESSAGE FROM JESUS ANGEL
SOME PEOPLE ARE HIRED IN THE
WORKPLACE TO BE INSTIGATORS
BULLIES AND TROUBLEMAKERS.
JESUS IS WATCHING THOSE PEOPLE
LIKE A HAWK. COOK UP ANY LIES, IT
WON'T STICK. JESUS IS STOP PLAYING
THE, DON'T ASSUME ANYTHING GAME.
HOSTILE ENVIRONMENT WAS USED ON
6/30/2022. WELCOME, TAKE A SEAT,
JESUS IS BEHIND EVERY SCENE.
FREEDOM OF RELIGION, AND FREEDOM OF
SPEECH ARE APART OF THIS FAMILY TREE.
WELCOME TO JESUS LABORATORY, THIS'S
NO CURSE, IT'S ALWAYS PATIENT FIRST.
LIFE IS MORE FUN, IF WE APPRECIATE AND
WELCOME JESUS SUN. ☀🗻🎴

Workplace Meeting Is going to sound
Like this in the Future.
Policies and Protocols still Stands.
Safety First and Patient First walks hands In Hands.
All complaints will be Tally in a Box for A Raffle Talk.
Love and Respect each other's Space.
Follow Code of Conduct. Take a Pizza 🍕
And A Donut 🍩 on your way in or Out.
This concludes this Meeting in 2023-2024
Smile to Regulate your Heart Rhythm ♪.
Now Breathe. PLB.

I HOPE IN THE FUTURE
JESUS WILL FIND ROOM
IN HIS HEART TO WRITE
AND PASS THIS BILL OF
RIGHTS IN THE WORKPLACE.
IF ANYONE CHOOSE TO LIE
ON MY ANGELS, GET FIRED OR
QUIT YOUR JOB IMMEDIATELY.
STAT.
IT'S CALLED THE PAULETTE BILL
TO FREEDOM OF SPEECH.
WELCOME, WELCOME, WELCOME.

THE NAKED TRUTH
IS WRITTEN BY AN ANGEL
BELIEVE IN YOURSELF FIRST.
THE WORLD AROUND YOU
IS A UNIVERSAL MIRROR
BE THE CHANGE THAT THE
WORLD NEEDS, NOT WHAT
THE WORLD WANTS.
SHALOM.
PLB.

The Naked truth
Twenty Eight years
To get the Invisible Dream
from finally Release me
To be an American Eagle
I am still Wondering What
To do with the Hummingbird
Belly. Smile America
The truth is What get us
To this Point.
We Were all born Naked.
Jeans will Now Show
the Wealth.
Shalom.

THIS WORLD IS A CRUEL PLACE
TRUST JESUS AND YOU WILL
ALWAYS BE SAFE.
SHALOM.
AMEN

AMERICA SAYS
IT TAKES MONEY
TO MAKE MONEY
JAMAICA AND THE
REST OF THE WORLD
COULD SAY!!
JESUS IS OUR MONEY.
IT TAKES ONE LOVE TO
FREE ALL MONEY.
SHALOM.

I HAVE FOUGHT
THE GOOD FIGHT
I HAVE FINISHED
THE RACE.
I HAVE KEPT THE
FAITH.
2 TIMOTHY 4:7
APRIL 7,1966
ONE OF JESUS
TRUE ANGEL
WAS BORN.
HER NAME IS AND
WAS PAULETTE.
THE NAKED TRUTH.

JESUS HAS STRATEGICALLY
WORK OVERTIME TO KEEP
ME SAFE FROM LIARS IN
AMERICA.
THEY VIEW ME UNDER THEIR
MICROSCOPE AS A TARGET.
THANK YOU JESUS FOR LIFE.
THIS'S THE NAKED TRUTH.
SHALOM.

RESPECT MY PRIVACY
AND MY SPACE. AND I
WILL DO THE SAME FOR
YOU. PRN.
Shalom ♥.

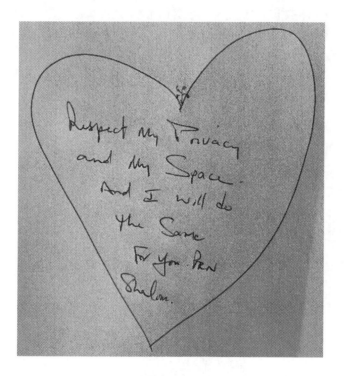

NATURES VALLEY KNOWS MY NAME.
PAIN AND ANGUISH SHOULD NEVER
BE THE SAME, FUN AND LAUGHTER
COULD BE A GAME. PLANT 🌱 THIS
DIAMOND OVER AGAIN. THE WORLD
DNA IS ON A STICK, SCOPE IN TO READ
JESUS ROYALTY PICK, DON'T FORGET YOUR
BRICK 🧱. BE THE GATEKEEPER WITH A
POETRY PACEMAKER. JESUS IS THE MARKETING DIRECTOR
FOREVER.
I DIDN'T HAVE TO GIVE HIM A QUOTA.
SO BEFORE YOU GO WALKING, STOP MY POEMS ARE
TALKING. HEALING FOR EVERY SOUL.
YES YOU'RE LOOKING BEAUTIFUL UNDER THIS WALKING
POET'S TREE. SAFE THE LAST DANCE FOR ME. WELCOME TO
NATURES VALLEY. IT'S TO LOVE AND BEHOLD, ON EVERY
ANNIVERSARY.
HAPPY BIRTHDAY BABY.

TAKE A GOOD LOOK
AT ME.
IF YOU TARGET ME IN THE
WORKPLACE. YOU WILL
BE TERMINATED WITH A
COST **$** FROM HEAVEN
THIS'S NO JOKE. IT'S
THE NAKED TRUTH.
TO EVERY BULLY BE A BUDDY
NOT A BULLY. TO EVERY
INSTIGATOR EAT MY PRAYER
FOR SUPPER. TO ALL TROUBLE
MAKERS STAY HOME AND MAKE
THE WORLD SAFER ON THE ROAD.
SHALOM.

WHEN I AM IN CRISIS
COVER MY HEAD TO
PROTECT MY DIGNITY.
LEND ME A HAND TO
REMOVE ALL PRIDE.
LOAN ME YOUR EMPATHY
SO I DON'T HAVE TO
FACE CRISIS ALONE.
LIFE IS A JOURNEY.
SHALOM.

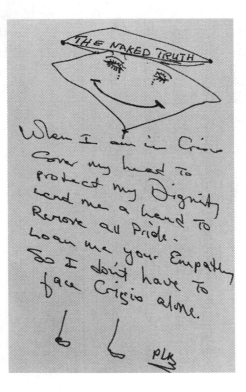

NEVER EXPECT TOO MUCH
NEVER ASSUME ANYTHING
NEVER ASK!! AND NEVER
DEMAND.
JUST LET THINGS BE.
IF IT WAS MEANT TO BE
IT WILL BE.
BE YOURSELF AND FEEL
FREE.
PLB.

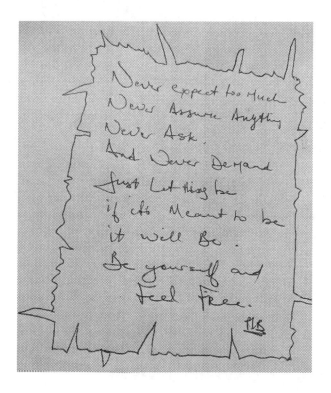

THE NAKED TRUTH
EVERYONE WAS BORN
NAKED. ENJOY LIFE'S
JOURNEY WITH EXTRA
ACCESSORIES. SHOES
CLOTHES, WIGS, BOTOX
FILLERS AND WHATEVER
ELSE, THAT FEELS MISSING.
FREEDOM LIVES WITHIN.
THIS'S WHY THE WORLD WAS
BORN NAKED. BUILD YOUR
HOUSE ON A ROCK, DRIVE YOUR
CAR WITH SAFETY FIRST. WALK
WITH FAITH AND CONSCIENCE BY
YOUR SIDE. FAMILY AND FRIENDS
LEARN TO LOVE EVERYBODY SPACE.
ALL LADIES WEAR RED TO BED.

PSALM 23: 1-6
THIS'S MY BREAD
AND BUTTER.
JESUS IS ALIVE.

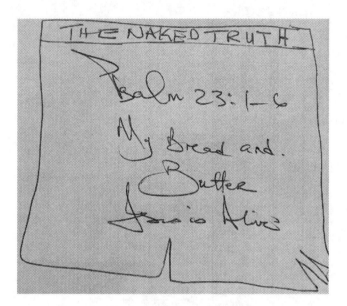

JESUS 2in1 MASK.
PATIENT FIRST
THEY'RE THE ONLY
ONE'S THAT'S
ALLOWED TO CURSE.
SO FLAP YOUR WINGS
AND WIGGLE YOUR TAILS.
THIS'S A FOREVER TASK
TO ALWAYS WEAR YOUR
TWO IN ONE MASK-
UPLIFTING IS NEVER A
WASTE. GIFTED1 IS IN A UPPER
CLASS TO CREATE THIS MASK. '2in1'

TODAY IS FULL OF POSSIBILITIES
USE YOUR OPEN MINDED KEY PRN
THE NAKED TRUTH.

YOU MUST BE WILLING
TO ACT TODAY
IN ORDER TO SUCCEED.
SMILE THEN ORDER
THE NAKED TRUTH.
MARKETING STRATEGIC
MOVE.

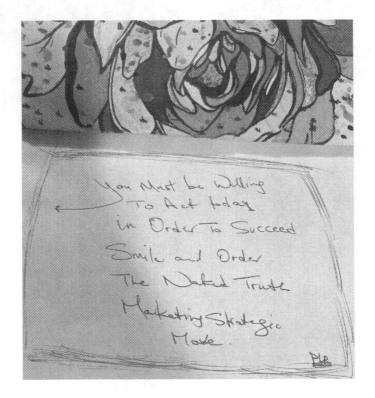

I AM MARRIED TO MY WRITING
I AM DEVOTED TO MY DREAMS.
I AM HAPPY TO BE ALIVE TODAY.
YAY!!
JESUS PROTECTS MY RIGHTS IN
AMERICA
FREEDOM IS FREE FOR ALL TO READ.
THE NAKED TRUTH.
JAMAICA ROOTS LIVES WITHIN.

If you're reading this Book
at this point you're aware
that we're
the future.
You cannot
invite me
without the
other.

The Naked Truth

PLB

I BECAME AN AMERICAN EAGLE
BECAUSE I DON'T WANT TO BE
A TARGET IN THE WORKPLACE
ANYMORE. SAFETY FIRST.

Amen.

PLANT THIS DIAMOND.
HISTORY WILL REPEAT ITSELF
OVER AND OVER AGAIN IN
AMERICA. PLANE CRASHES
ROCKETS MALFUNCTION
SENSELESS SHOOTINGS
ARE JUST A FEW. CHAOS
EVERYWHERE, CONFUSION
AND PAIN, EATING AWAY
FAMILY MEMBRANES. LEAVING
STRESS AND INFECTION TO SET
IN MOTION. JUSTICE SYSTEM
FLIP AND RE-FLIP THE SCRIPT
TO COVER UP CORRUPTIONS.
ONLY JESUS CAN SAVE US.
PLANT THIS DIAMOND IS A
WRITTEN BOOK. HEALING
FROM INSIDE OUT.
SHALOM.

IN THE FUTURE I WANT TO WALK
INTO A ROOM FILLED WITH CANDLES.
CELEBRATING LIGHT A CANDLE WITH
JESUS MOMENT. THEN WHEN I OPEN
MY EYES, I WON'T BE SHOCK TO SEE
THAT THE ENTIRE WORLD IS CELEBRATING
THIS MOMENT WITH JESUS AND PAULETTE.
DON'T LOOK AROUND THAT'S ME.
ENJOY THE NAKED TRUTH WITH A SMILE.
SHALOM.

THE WORLD IS LIKE AN
ELASTIC BAND, YOU CAN
STRETCH IT IN ANY DIRECTION
POSSIBLE. STAY FOCUS IN THE
WORLD OF MARKETING.

EVERYTHING IS A TEST IN THE EYES
OF THE #GIFTED1.

FOCUS ON THE SOLUTION AND NEVER
THE PROBLEM.
Shalom.

THE NAKED TRUTH MEANS:
EVEN THOUGH IT'S
TRUE IN JAMAICA
AMERICA OVERLOOK
THE TRUTH TO
REVIEW A HIGHER
POWER.
PLB

Paulette Lewis-Brown strongly believes that Jesus is her Markcting Director, in this far from puurfect world. She devoted abundance of her time to her writing. Her faith guides her along lifes journey, Jesus always leads the way.

America will Accomodate the world but do they know
how to Welcome all of Gods Creations?

THE NAKED TRUTH will be a legacy, rooted up from Jamaica
to share with the Universe. United we stand, out of many we're
one. No man is an island, no one should feel alone. Eternal father
give us hope to forgive and bless every HEART. When the world
fall apart, our legacy stands to carry on. Welcome to America
after twenty eight years. Welcome home, sweet home.
You're now one of us. Here's your A+_.

Shalom

I AM JESUS CHATTER BOX BIRD.
AN EAGLE WITH AN HUMMINGBIRD
BELLY.

PLB.

EDGAR IS AN ONLY CHILD
HE'S MY AMERICAN PRIDE
AND JOY. SMILE AND ENJOY
MY 15th BOOK. 🏠
THE NAKED TRUTH.
SHALOM. 🕊

PEACE BE WITH YOU.

Printed in the United States
by Baker & Taylor Publisher Services